The
World's Best
Light-Bulb
Jokes

In this series:

The World's Best Dirty Jokes
More of the World's Best Dirty Jokes
Still More of the World's Best Dirty Jokes
The World's Best Irish Jokes
More of the World's Best Irish Jokes
Still More of the World's Best Irish Jokes
The World's Best Jewish Jokes
More of the World's Best Jewish Jokes
The World's Best Doctor Jokes
More of the World's Best Doctor Jokes
The World's Best Dirty Stories
The World's Best Dirty Limericks
The World's Best Dirty Songs
The World's Best Business Jokes
The World's Best Mother-in-Law Jokes
The World's Best Fishing Jokes
The World's Best Salesman Jokes
The World's Best Golf Jokes
More of the World's Best Golf Jokes
The World's Best Scottish Jokes
The World's Best Football Jokes
The World's Best Cricket Jokes
The World's Best Lawyer Jokes
The World's Best Holiday Jokes
The World's Best Acting Jokes
The World's Best Drinking Jokes
More of the World's Best Drinking Jokes
The World's Best Gardening Jokes
The World's Best Motoring Jokes
The World's Best Marriage Jokes
The World's Best After-Dinner Jokes
The World's Best Skiing Jokes
The World's Best Boss Jokes

The World's Best Light-Bulb Jokes

Cathy Hopkins and Edward Phillips

Illustrated by Frank Dickens

HarperCollins*Publishers*

HarperCollins*Publishers*
77–85 Fulham Palace Road,
Hammersmith, London W6 8JB

A Paperback Original 1995
1 3 5 7 9 8 6 4 2

A catalogue record for this book
is available from the British Library

ISBN 0 00 638461 7

Photoset in Goudy Old Style by
Rowland Phototypesetting Limited
Bury St Edmunds, Suffolk

Printed in Great Britain by
HarperCollinsManufacturing Glasgow

With grateful thanks to Christine Kelly
and David Pugh for their contributions, and
to Laury King for his permission to use items
from the *Mensa Newsletter*.

How many SOCIOLOGISTS does it take to change a light-bulb?

It isn't the light-bulb that needs changing, it's the whole system.

How many PRISON WARDERS does it take to change a light-bulb?

Two. One screw to screw in the bulb and another screw to screw the first screw if he screws up.

How many GREEK GODS does it take to change a light-bulb?

Two. One to hold the bulb and one to rotate the planet.

The man generally accredited with the invention of the light-bulb is Thomas Alva Edison, the American inventor (1847–1931). Do you realize that if it wasn't for that great man, we'd all have to watch television by candlelight?

How many BORN-AGAIN CHRISTIANS does it take to change a light-bulb?

Ten. One to change the bulb and nine to rush out into the street shouting, 'I've seen the light! I've seen the light!'

How many CORONERS does it take to change a light-bulb?

Two. One to change the bulb and one to pronounce the old bulb dead from natural causes and sign the certificate.

How many GERMANS does it take to change a light-bulb?

'Ve ask the questions!'

How many MAFIA MEN does it take to change a light-bulb?

Two. One to change the bulb and the other to shoot the witnesses.

How many FRENCHMEN does it take to change a light-bulb?

Four. One to change the bulb and three to open the wine.

How many FEMINISTS does it take to change a light-bulb?

'Just one, you sexist pig – and it's not funny!'

How many PROCRASTINATORS does it take to change a light-bulb?

Just one – but would it be all right if he did it next week?

What do you find printed on an Irish light-bulb?

On the top end: SCREW IN OTHER END.
On the bottom end: SEE OTHER END FOR
                         INSTRUCTIONS.

How many BOURGEOIS CAPITALIST PIGS does it take to change a light-bulb?

Two. One to exploit the proletariat and one to control the means of production.

How many SUPERMODELS does it take to change a light-bulb?

None. 'What do you want me to do – ruin my nail-polish?'

How many JEWISH BUSINESSMEN does it take to change a light-bulb?

Two. One to find a new one at a bargain price and one to sell the old one at a profit.

In the old days of the Soviet Union, the Russians used to claim that everything had been invented by the glorious scientists of the USSR. Russia was the only country in the world where a scientist invented the light-bulb while working by the light of one.

How many WHITEHALL BUREAUCRATS does it take to change a light-bulb?

None. 'We contract out for things like that.'

How many JEWISH MOTHERS does it take to change a light-bulb?

None. 'It's all right, don't worry – I'll just sit here in the dark, alone!'

How many MIDGETS does it take to change a light-bulb?

Only one. As long as he can find a couple more to put him up to it.

How many TWELFTH-CENTURY WORKMEN did it take to change a light-bulb?

None. There were no light-bulbs then – it was the Dark Ages.

How many SCHOOLTEACHERS does it take to change a light-bulb?

If at home – one. If at school – six.

How many POLICEMEN does it take to change a light-bulb?

None. It turned itself in.

An American company has just invented a new light-bulb that will last up to thirty years. This is longer than the average marriage lasts today. Just think of it. You could be on your third marriage and still be on your first light-bulb.

How many EDITORS does it take to change a light-bulb?

Two. One to change the bulb and one to send out a rejection slip to the old bulb.

How many PESSIMISTS does it take to change a light-bulb?

'Oh, what's the use? It'll only blow again.'

How many ROBOTS does it take to change a light-bulb?

Two. One to change the bulb and one to say, 'Not in my left ear, stupid! In my right ear!'

How many STUDENTS does it take to change a light-bulb?

Three hundred. One to change the bulb and 299 to picket the university demanding higher grants for heating and lighting.

Did you hear the one about the man who walked into a psychiatrist's office with a light-bulb screwed into each of his ears? He said, 'Doctor, I want to talk to you about my brother.'

How many FILM DIRECTORS does it take to change a light-bulb?

'I don't care how many it takes, what it costs, or how you do it – JUST GET IT CHANGED, OK!!!'

How many GAY RIGHTS ACTIVISTS does it take to change a light-bulb?

Why should the light-bulb have to change? Why can't society accept it as it is?

How many MISSIONARIES does it take to change a light-bulb?

Five hundred and one. One to change the bulb and 500 to go out and try to persuade everybody else to change theirs too.

How many UNIVERSITY GRADUATES does it take to change a light-bulb?

Only one – but it can take him up to seven years.

How many DEAF PEOPLE does it take to change a light-bulb?

'Pardon?'

How many BORING PEOPLE does it take to change a light-bulb?

One.

'Doctor, every morning at breakfast, my husband imagines he's a light-bulb.'
   'Have you tried to convince him he isn't?'
   'What, and eat in the dark?'

How many JEWISH WIVES does it take to change a light-bulb?

Five. Four to bitch about it and one to get her husband to do it.

How many GOVERNMENT MINISTERS does it take to change a light-bulb?

Government ministers never change light-bulbs. They prefer to keep the public in the dark.

How many ANTI-ABORTIONISTS does it take to screw in a light-bulb?

Ten. One to screw in the bulb and nine to maintain that the bulb was lit from the moment they began screwing.

How many PROSTITUTES does it take to change a light-bulb?

Two. One to change the bulb and one to paint the new one red.

How many CALIFORNIANS does it take to change a light-bulb?

Ninety-five. One to change the bulb, and ninety-four to share the experience.

An electrician was changing a light-bulb in the front room of a suburban house.

'The ceiling's very high here,' he remarked to the householder.

'Yes, it's the wife,' said the householder. 'She wanted two rooms knocked into one.'

How many GORILLAS does it take to change a light-bulb?

One. But it takes a hell of a lot of light-bulbs.

How many PUNK ROCKERS does it take to change a light-bulb?

Two. One to change the bulb and one to kick the chair out from under him.

How many GOVERNMENT OFFICIALS does it take to change a light-bulb?

One – but he'll need twenty-four private outside consultants to advise him.

How many ACID-HEADS does it take to change a light-bulb?

'None, man, none! The light-bulb changes itself – first into a supernova and then into another universe.'

How many FEMINISTS does it take to change a light-bulb?

Five. One to change the bulb, two to discuss the violation of the socket and two to wish secretly that they were the socket.

What is a right-bulb?
A Japanese light-bulb.

How many SCHIZOPHRENICS does it take to change a light-bulb?

One . . . or two, depending on the time of his last medication.

How many NEW YORKERS does it take to change a light-bulb?

'None of your goddamn business!'

How many MI5 AGENTS does it take to change a light-bulb?

'Why do you want to know? Who are you working for? What are the names of your associates? Who's paying you for this information?'

How many CLOWNS does it take to change a light-bulb?

Five. One to change the bulb and set himself on fire, one to throw a bucket of water over him, two to crash into the ladder and knock it over and one to spray the lot of them with a fire extinguisher.

Of course, although Edison invented the light-bulb, it was the chap who invented the meter who made all the money.

How many THOUGHT POLICE does it take to change a light-bulb?

None. There never was any light-bulb.

How many CELIBATES does it take to screw in a light-bulb?

Celibates never screw anything.

How many BLACKPOOL TOWN COUNCILLORS does it take to change a light-bulb?

One – and Cilla Black to switch it on afterwards.

How many NEW YORKERS does it take to change a light-bulb?

Two hundred and one. One to change the bulb and 200 to watch it happen without trying to stop it.

How many OPINION POLLSTERS does it take to change a light-bulb?

Ten. One to change the bulb and nine to stop people in the street and ask them whether the bulb should have been changed in the first place, and what are the advantages, if any, of the new one.

How many CABINET MINISTERS does it take to change a light-bulb?

Two. One to assure the public that everything possible is being done, while the other screws the bulb into the hot-water tap.

A man was polishing a light-bulb before inserting it into the socket, when there was a big flash and a genie appeared before him. 'I am the genie of the light-bulb,' he said. 'I will answer any three questions for you – but only three. Do you have three questions you would like to ask?'

'Who? Me?' said the man.

'Yes, you,' said the genie. 'Now, what is your third question?'

How many WOMEN SUFFERING FROM PMT does it take to change a light-bulb?

'How the hell should I know! Haven't you got anything better to do than go around asking stupid questions?'

How many SCOTSMEN does it take to change a light-bulb?

Scotsmen don't change light-bulbs. It's cheaper to sit in the dark.

How many MORMONS does it take to change a light-bulb?

One man and thirty women. The man changes the bulb, while one wife holds the ladder, one wife hands him up the new bulb, one wife takes the old bulb, one wife stands by the switch, one wife . . .

How many LOCAL COUNCILLORS does it take to change a light-bulb?

Forty-four. One to change the bulb and forty-three to organize a £50,000 trip to the Bahamas to see how light-bulbs are changed in the Caribbean.

I was staying at a hotel in Manchester last week, and I called up the manager and told him the room was too cold. So he put a larger bulb in the lamp.

How many PRIMA DONNAS does it take to change a light-bulb?

'Prima donnas don't change anything – ever! Right?'

How many PAKISTANIS does it take to change a light-bulb?

One – but it takes the whole village a year to save up to buy the bulb.

How many TERRORISTS does it take to change a light-bulb?

Twenty. One to change the bulb and nineteen to organize the diversion.

How many ANGLERS does it take to change a light-bulb?

Three. One to change the bulb and two to bore everybody down at their local with stories about how big the old one was.

How many GROUP 4 SECURITY MEN does it take to change a light-bulb?

Five. They never get around to changing the light-bulb, but it takes five of them to write a report explaining that they had the new light-bulb under guard in a locked van when they left the office – but when they arrived, it had somehow disappeared.

How many WAITERS does it take to change a light-bulb?

None. Even a burned-out bulb can't catch a waiter's eye.

Psychiatrist: 'So what seems to be the trouble?'
Patient: 'Well, everybody thinks I'm crazy – just because I have this thing about light-bulbs.'
Psychiatrist: 'That doesn't sound so bad. I quite like light-bulbs myself.'
Patient: 'You do? How do you like yours – fried, boiled or poached?'

How many DEMOLITION WORKERS does it take to change a light-bulb?

Just one – if he's got a big enough sledgehammer.

How many MEMBERS OF A BOARD OF MANAGERS does it take to change a light-bulb?

This topic was resumed from last month's Board Meeting and after further discussion was postponed until next month pending further research.

How many NUDISTS does it take to change a light-bulb?

Two. It only takes one to change the bulb, but it takes another one to hand him up the new bulb because the first one has nowhere to put it while he climbs the ladder.

How many STRAIGHT SAN FRANCISCANS does it take to change a light-bulb?

Both of them.

Did you hear about the glass-blower who got hiccups? Before anyone could stop him, he'd turned out 498 sixty-watt light-bulbs.

How many LAGER LOUTS does it take to screw in a light-bulb?

Just one. Lager louts will screw anything.

How many RUSSIANS does it take to change a light-bulb?

Three. One who knows about electricity, one who can read the instructions and one to keep an eye on the two dangerous intellectuals.

How many ICI EXECUTIVES does it take to change a light-bulb?

This information is classified and is only available to qualified research and development bodies on payment of a licence fee and completion of a royalties agreement.

How many FEMINISTS does it take to change a light-bulb?

Two. One to change the bulb and one to write an article about how it feels from a woman's point of view.

How many RED INDIANS does it take to change a light-bulb?

Twenty-five. One to change the bulb and twenty-four to do a dance of thanksgiving to Osram, the Great God of Light.

How many ROAD WORKERS does it take to change a light-bulb?

Ten. One to change the bulb and nine to lean on their shovels and watch.

Did you hear about the Irish electrician who climbed up a sixteen-foot ladder to change a light-bulb and ended up in hospital? He stepped back to admire his work.

How many SHOP STEWARDS does it take to change a light-bulb?

One. But he never changes just the one bulb. 'If we change one, then they'll all have to be changed. One out, all out!'

How many MULTI-MILLIONAIRES does it take to change a light-bulb?

Multi-millionaires don't change light-bulbs, they change apartments.

How many SURREALISTS does it take to change a light-bulb?

To get to the other side.

How many NEW YORKERS does it take to change a light-bulb?

Fifty. One to change the bulb and forty-nine policemen to make sure he isn't mugged on his way up the ladder.

A man once left home to seek fame and fortune. He was away for ten years, and all that time his loving wife kept a light burning in the front-room window to welcome him back on his return. When he did finally get home, they had to sell the house because they had an electricity bill for £19,856.

How many YUPPIES does it take to screw in a light-bulb?

None. Yuppies only screw in jacuzzis.

How many PHOTOGRAPHERS does it take to change a light-bulb?

Only one – but he's got to wait until the light is better.

How many BARRISTERS does it take to change a light-bulb?

'Where the term "light-bulb" refers to an ordinary appliance used solely and exclusively for the purposes of domestic illumination, notwithstanding that such appliance may also be used for purposes under the Act not wholly or exclusively domestic, and where there is a prima facie case for supposing that such bulb or bulbs are in compliance with an ad hoc definition of . . .'

'For God's sake, how many?'

'One!'

How many POLICEMEN does it take to change a light-bulb?

Just one – but he's never around when you want him.

How many GARAGE MECHANICS does it take to change a light-bulb?

Six. One to polish the fitting, one to replace the fitting after it's been polished ('It was looking very worn, sir'), one to get a new light-bulb, one to go back to the garage to get the right new light-bulb, one to try and change the bulb, without success and one to phone later and say, 'It'll take a couple of weeks, squire – and you won't get much change of a hundred quid.'

How many FORTUNE-TELLERS does it take to change a light-bulb?

Two. One to change the bulb and one to read the tarot cards to find out how long the new bulb will last.

Did you know that light travels from the sun to the earth at a speed of 186,000 miles per second?
Of course, it's downhill all the way.

How many BUS CONDUCTORS does it take to change a light-bulb?

Are you kidding? They won't even change a five-pound note.

How many BASKETBALL PLAYERS does it take to change a light-bulb?

Only one – and he doesn't need a ladder, either.

How many BALLET DANCERS does it take to change a light-bulb?

Just one, provided he can execute a sauté or a jeté to reach the bulb. Otherwise two, to execute a pas de deux with lift.

How many CARTOONISTS does it take to change a light-bulb?

Two. One to change the bulb and one to draw a picture of a man with a light-bulb in a 'balloon' over his head, exclaiming, 'I've just had a brilliant idea!'

A Martian visiting earth went into a hardware shop to buy a light-bulb. 'Don't bother wrapping it,' he said. 'I'll eat it here.'

How many ESSEX GIRLS does it take to change a light-bulb?

Essex girls don't change light-bulbs. They just shout, 'Oy, Wayne! Get over 'ere!'

How many CIVIL SERVANTS does it take to change a light-bulb?

Fifty. One to insert the bulb and forty-nine to screw the whole thing up.

How many LUMBERJACKS does it take to change a light-bulb?

One – but he has to use a chain saw.

How many BLACKS does it take to change a light-bulb?

Ten. One to change the bulb and nine to provide the back-up music.

How many CENSORS does it take to change a light-bulb?

————. One to ——— the ———, one to ——————— and ——————— to ———————————.

How many IRANIANS does it take to change a light-bulb?

One thousand and one. One to change the bulb and a thousand to rebuild the power station.

What does an Irish photographer do with a burned-out light-bulb?
He saves it to use in his dark-room.

How many PUBLIC RELATIONS MEN does it take to change a light-bulb?

Seventeen. One to create the event, three to send out the invitations and the rest to hand round the drinks.

How many JUDGES does it take to change a light-bulb?

'*What is a light-bulb?*'

How many SPACEMEN does it take to change a light-bulb?

Two. One to panic and one to call Mission Control and shout, 'Mayday! Mayday! We have a malfunction in the overhead console illumination control panel! Should we abort?'

How many MOTOR MECHANICS does it take to change a light-bulb?

Four. One to try to force it in with a hammer and three to go out for more bulbs.

Edison worked long and hard for years to find the right sort of filament for his light-bulb. And then, one winter's night, round about midnight, he found it. Mrs Edison was already in bed when Edison rushed into the bedroom, holding his precious light-bulb aloft, and shouting excitedly, 'Look, dear, I've done it! I've finally done it!'

'Well done, dear,' said his wife. 'Now, for goodness' sake, put the light out and come to bed!'

How many WOMEN does it take to change a light-bulb?

Six. One to be elected spokeswoman and the other five to coax her into asking the nearest man to change it for her.

How many VENTRILOQUISTS does it take to change a light-bulb?

Two. One to change the gulg and one to gold the gottom of the lagger.

How many INMATES OF AN OLD PEOPLE'S HOME does it take to change a light-bulb?

Ten. One to change the bulb and nine to complain about how much lovelier the old one was.

How many ARGUMENTATIVE PEOPLE does it take to change a light-bulb?

None. 'Are you sure it isn't the socket? Maybe it isn't screwed in properly – or perhaps you're using too strong a bulb. Why don't you call in an electrician . . . ?'

How many MEMBERS OF THE EUROPEAN PARLIAMENT does it take to change a light-bulb?

Fifty. One to change the bulb and forty-nine to register a veto and protest that, on the grounds of British sovereignty, the British Parliament, and not Brussels, dominated as it is by French and German interests, should have the right to determine whether the light-bulb needed changing or not.

When an Irish electrician is given the job of fitting a new light-bulb, why is it not a good idea to give him a tea-break?

It takes too long to re-train him.

How many VANDALS does it take to change a light-bulb?

Two. One to put the new light-bulb in and the other to smash it.

How many HARLEY STREET PSYCHIATRISTS does it take to change a light-bulb?

Only one – but it will take a very long time and will be very expensive.

How many PEOPLE WITH A STIFF NECK does it take to change a light-bulb?

None. They can't look up to see what they're doing.

How many TRADE UNION OFFICIALS does it take to change a light-bulb?

Ten. One to change the bulb and nine to negotiate a 15 per cent pay rise and the upgrading of the job from unskilled to semi-skilled status.

How many UNDERGROUND TRAIN STAFF does it take to change a light-bulb?

Two. One to change the bulb and one to apologize for the delay.

Did you hear about the absent-minded professor who screwed his wife in the bedroom and took a light-bulb out to dinner?

How many MAGICIANS does it take to change a light-bulb?

It depends on what you want to change it into.

How many AMPUTEES does it take to change a light-bulb?

Just one – as long as he can get someone to lend him a hand.

'Do you know how many MUSICIANS it takes to change a light-bulb?

'No – but if you hum a few bars, I'll improvise it.'

How many MINI-CAB DRIVERS does it take to change a light-bulb?

One – but he has to get on to the office and ask for directions before he can get to the socket.

How many IRAQI ARMS EXPERTS does it take to change a light-bulb?

Two. One to change the bulb and one to ask the Russian advisor which way to turn it.

How many MACHO MEN does it take to change a light-bulb?

None. Macho men aren't afraid of the dark.

How many LAWYERS does it take to change a light-bulb?

Three. One to change the bulb, one to write out the bill and one to put it in the post.

The patient was finally cured. At the end of his last interview, the psychiatrist asked him about his plans for the future.

'Well,' said the patient, 'as you know, I've got a First Class Honours Degree in Science and Engineering, so the field is wide open. I might go into industry, or join one of the ministries; or I could go into consultancy or research. I could try teaching or writing. On the other hand, of course, I might just go back to being a light-bulb.'

How many LUNATICS does it take to change a light-bulb?

Two. One to change the bulb and one to tell him to be sure to stick his fingers in the empty socket first to make certain the electricity is coming through all right.

How many EXISTENTIALIST POETS does it take to change a light-bulb?

Two. One to screw it in and one to write a poem about how the new light-bulb symbolizes subjective reality surrounded by the cosmic emptiness of objective awareness in a material universe which consists basically of eternal nothingness.

How many CLAIRVOYANTS does it take to change a light-bulb?

Only one – but she'll change it twenty-four hours before the old one expires.

Two inmates were trying to escape from a mental home. They had got as far as the outer wall but could see no way of getting over it. Then one of them noticed a searchlight at the top of a guard tower, and he said, 'If we can get up that tower, I'll turn the light on and point the beam towards the ground, then you can slide down it!'

'You must be joking!' said his mate. 'I know what your game is. You'll let me get half-way down the beam and then you'll switch the light off!'

How many MOTHS does it take to change a light-bulb?

One hundred. One to change the bulb and ninety-nine to yell. 'Look out! Here we come! Wheeeeeee!' CRASH!

How many DOCTORS does it take to change a light-bulb?

That depends on whether or not it belongs to BUPA.

How many ACTORS does it take to change a light-bulb?

One – but he also needs a director, an assistant director, two stage managers and a choreographer to tell him where to stand to catch the light.

How many IDIOTS WHO ASK STUPID QUESTIONS does it take to change a light-bulb?

'Change it to what?'

How many HAMPSTEAD LIBERALS does it take to change a light-bulb?

None – after all, someone might want to sit in the dark.

How many AMBULANCE DRIVERS does it take to change a light-bulb?

Three. One to take out the old bulb and two to turn up an hour and a half later in the ambulance with the new one and explain that it was a very busy night, and they were short-staffed, and the nearest available ambulance was at Sheerness, and . . .

A psychologist was engaged in a series of therapy sessions with a confirmed alcoholic. Reporting to his supervisor, he said, 'I'm making progress, but there is one thing that worries me. I'm doing standard conditioning; every time the patient reaches for a glass of whisky, he receives an electric shock. But it doesn't seem to be working out as it should. Before he can take a drink now, he has to stick two fingers in the nearest light socket.'

How many THEATRE CRITICS does it take to change a light-bulb?

Two. One to change the bulb and one to write a review saying, 'One of the most lacklustre and pointless evenings I have spent for many a month . . .'

How many JAPANESE INDUSTRIALISTS does it take to change a light-bulb?

Three. One to make sure the new bulb is not of foreign manufacture, one to change the bulb and one to investigate the export potential of the old bulb.

How many PHOTOGRAPHIC SALES REPS does it take to screw in a new light-bulb?

None. Photographic sales reps don't screw light-bulbs, they screw photographers.

How many ZEN MASTERS does it take to change a light-bulb?

Two. One to change it and one not to change it.

A worried-looking woman went to see a psychiatrist and said to the doctor, 'I want to talk to you about my husband. He's convinced he's a refrigerator.'

'Well, that's nothing to worry about,' said the psychiatrist. 'I would say that's quite a harmless obsession.'

'Yes, but the thing is,' said the woman, 'he sleeps with his mouth open and the little light keeps me awake at night.'

How many ZEN BUDDHISTS does it take to change a light-bulb?

A Zen Buddhist is part of the Universe. A light-bulb is part of the Universe. The Universe encompasses everything. Every part of the Universe is also the whole Universe. Therefore a Zen Buddhist is the light-bulb.

How many ADVERTISING ART DIRECTORS does it take to change a light-bulb?

None. Advertising art directors don't change anything.

How many PENTAGON GULF WAR STAFF does it take to change a light-bulb?

'We have no information at this time due to the fact that . . .'

How many ARABS does it take to change a light-bulb?

Three. One to hold the bulb and two to turn the stool — but they also need a foreign advisor to tell them the old one has burnt out.

How many BUILDING CONSTRUCTION WORKERS does it take to change a light-bulb?

'Sorry, it's not my job, mate.'

An electrician was changing a light-bulb in the kitchen one morning when the lady of the house walked in, wearing nothing but a skimpy negligee. With a sly smile, she said softly, 'Would you like a bunk-up?'

'No thanks, lady,' said the electrician. 'I've brought my own ladder.'

How many NUCLEAR PROTESTORS does it take to change a light-bulb?

A hundred. One to change the bulb and ninety-nine to mount a demonstration outside the nuclear power station that produces the electricity that powers it.

How many BLONDE BIMBOS does it take to change a light-bulb?

One. She just holds it up to the socket and waits for the world to revolve around her.

How many US PRESIDENTS does it take to change a light-bulb?

One – plus 297 police, federal agents, CIA, FBI, Treasury officials and secret service men to make sure he isn't assassinated while he's doing it.

How many CIVIL SERVANTS does it take to change a light-bulb?

A hundred. One to change the bulb and ninety-nine to make out the necessary documentation.

How many PLUMBERS does it take to change a light-bulb?

Two. One to take out the old bulb and one to go back to the office to fetch the new one.

Ted: 'I came home unexpectedly last night and caught my wife on the sofa with another man. But I got even with him.'

Fred: 'What did you do?'

Ted: 'I turned out the light so he couldn't see what he was doing!'

How many ENGLAND FOOTBALLERS does it take to change a light-bulb?

Only one to actually change the bulb – but fifty-seven sports commentators and 'experts' are also needed, to discuss, analyse, replay the highlights of the action, talk about former great light-bulb changers (especially German, Argentinian and Brazilian) and argue about whether Stanley Matthews or Bobby Charlton would have done it better – all carefully documented by the BBC for five or six hours each day.

How many NIHILISTS does it take to change a light-bulb?

None. There's nothing to change.

How many DETECTIVES does it take to change a light-bulb?

Five. One to change the bulb, one to dust the old bulb for fingerprints, one to photograph the scene of the incident, one to question the witnesses and one to insist that no brutality was involved.

How many SCIENTIFIC RESEARCH AND DEVELOPMENT EXPERTS does it take to change a light-bulb?

One – provided there's an engineer around to explain how to do it.

How many DENTISTS does it take to change a light-bulb?

Only one. And he says, 'I'm afraid we can't save this one – it'll have to come out.'

How many JUNIOR DOCTORS does it take to change a light-bulb?

Just one – but he's too knackered to do it.

Did you hear about the Irishman who bought a long-life light-bulb? The manufacturers claimed that it would last for a hundred years and he wanted to see if it was true.

How many SUN REPORTERS does it take to change a light-bulb?

Only one – but he'll tell everybody about it.

How many ADVERTISING EXECUTIVES does it take to change a light-bulb?

Ten. One to change the bulb and nine to get the bar tab up to a respectable level.

How many ABSENT-MINDED PROFESSORS does it take to change a light-bulb?

Six. They never actually get it changed – they just stand around arguing about what they came in for in the first place.

How many BUSINESS EXECUTIVES does it take to change a light-bulb?

'Er . . . he's in a meeting right now . . . I'll get him to call you back.'

How many ESKIMOS does it take to change a light-bulb?

Two. One to change the bulb and one to say, 'That bulb's guaranteed for six months so it should last us through the night.'

A Frenchman, a German and an Englishman were arguing about which of their respective languages was the best.

The Frenchman said, 'French is the language of romance, the most beautiful language in the world.'

The German said, 'German is the language of science and technology, the language most fitted to the needs of the twentieth century.'

And the Englishman said, 'Nonsense! There's only one decent language, and that's English. We English say what we mean – no messing about. Take this for instance.' He held up a light-bulb. 'You Frenchmen call it an *ampoule*. And you Germans call it a *glühbirne*. We in England simply call it a light-bulb, which, after all, is precisely what it is.'

How many CIVIL SERVANTS does it take to change a light-bulb?

One to notice the burned-out bulb, one departmental head to authorize the requisition, one secretary to type out the requisition, three filing clerks to file the copies, a messenger to deliver the requisition to the purchasing department, a supervisor to authorize the purchase of the new bulb . . .

How many POLITICIANS does it take to change a light-bulb?

'The Government is well aware of the situation and we are setting up a committee to look into the possibility of . . .'

How many MATHEMATICIANS does it take to change a light-bulb?

$2^3 + 104 + \sqrt{16} - (10^2 + 10) - (2 \times 2.5)$.

How many BUS DRIVERS does it take to change a light-bulb?

Only one – but he never changes one light-bulb at a time. He always changes at least four or five, all at once, after you've been waiting for ages.

How many SPANISH HOTELIERS does it take to change a light-bulb?

'Change the light-bulb? We haven't even finished the hotel yet!'

A patient in a mental home was firmly convinced that he had swallowed a light-bulb and all the efforts of the team of psychiatrists to convince him otherwise were to no avail. Finally the chief psychiatrist tried one last trick. He put the patient to bed under heavy sedation and then unscrewed the light-bulb from the bedside lamp. He then laid the bulb carefully on the patient's chest. Presently the patient came round from the anaesthetic and the psychiatrist said, 'Nothing to worry about now, Mr Smith. We've managed to remove the light-bulb surgically!'

The patient picked the light-bulb up and examined it carefully. Then he looked up and said scornfully, 'You must think I'm stupid! This is a forty-watt plain. The one I swallowed was a hundred-watt pearl!'

How many UNDERTAKERS does it take to change a light-bulb?

Nine. One to change the bulb and eight to carry the dead one out in a pine box.

How many SEX THERAPISTS does it take to change a light-bulb?

Two. One to screw it in and one to tell him he's screwing it in the wrong way.

How many THRILLER WRITERS does it take to screw in a light-bulb?

Two. One to screw it in most of the way and the other to give it a surprising twist at the end.

How many MASOCHISTS does it take to change a light-bulb?

Two. One to change the bulb and one to stick his fingers in the socket to see if the electricity is coming through OK.

Two Irish electricians were engaged in changing a light-bulb. One of them suddenly shouted, 'Don't come down the ladder, Brendan – I've just taken it away!'

How many DISC JOCKEYS does it take to change a light-bulb?

Two. One to change the bulb and one to scream, 'Fantabuloso! Abso-mega-lutely brilliantissimo!'

How many TEENAGERS does it take to change a light-bulb?

'Do it yourself – it's your house! What am I, some sort of personal slave or something!'

How many ACCOUNTANTS does it take to change a light-bulb?

'What kind of answer did you have in mind?'

How many HOSPITAL ADMINISTRATORS does it take to change a light-bulb?

'Sorry, but that item has been cut from the budget.'

How many NEW PARENTS does it take to change a light-bulb?

Two. One to say, 'It's your turn to get up and change it, dear,' and one to do it.

How many MASSAGE PARLOUR GIRLS does it take to change a light-bulb?

'Whatever turns you on, ducky.'

Why is an Essex Girl like a twenty-watt light-bulb?
Neither of them is very bright.

How many FIREMEN does it take to change a light-bulb in a front hallway?

Five. One to change the bulb and four to smash down the front door to gain entry.

How many HOME OFFICE OFFICIALS does it take to change a light-bulb?

Twenty. One to screw it up and nineteen to draft the cover-up statement.

How many BLIND PEOPLE does it take to change
a light-bulb?

It depends whether the switch is on or off.

How many HAIRDRESSERS does it take to change a light-
bulb?

*Five. One to change the bulb and four to stand around
admiringly and say, 'Fabulous, Gary!'*

What is black and frizzled and hangs from the ceiling?
An Irish electrician.

How many ESSEX GIRLS does it take to screw in a light-
bulb?

None. Essex Girls only screw in Ford Sierras.

How many JUGGLERS does it take to change a
light-bulb?

One – but he needs a minimum of three bulbs.

How many LIGHTHOUSE-KEEPERS does it take to
change a light-bulb?

At least ten. Have you seen the size of their light-bulbs?

How many COUNTRY MUSIC SONG-WRITERS does it take to change a light-bulb?

Six. One to change the bulb and five to write about how much they miss the old one.

How many NEW MOTHERS does it take to change a light-bulb?

Only one – but she changes it every four hours, or whenever it gets dirty.

How many ELEPHANTS does it take to change a light-bulb?

They never do. Elephants are too heavy for light work.

'You got home early from your date last night. What happened?'
'Well, we went out for dinner and afterwards she invited me up to her place. We had a couple of drinks and she put some soft music on the cassette player – and then she reached over and turned out the light.'
'So?'
'Well, I can take a hint. I went home.'

How many AIR HOSTESSES does it take to change a light-bulb?

Three. One to explain the procedure, one to demonstrate it in mime and one to actually do it.

How many SWORD-SWALLOWERS does it take to change a light-bulb?

Two. One to change the bulb and one to swallow the old one.

How many ANTIQUE DEALERS does it take to change a light-bulb?

Two. One to change the bulb and one to preserve the old bulb and sell it as an Edison original.

How many ROYAL SHAKESPEARE COMPANY ACTORS does it take to change a light-bulb?

One. RSC actors don't like to share the spotlight.

A group of mental patients was engaged in some therapeutic work in the basement of the institution. When the superintendent came round, he saw that they were all busy at the carpentry benches and lathes, except for one inmate who was hanging by his ankles from the ceiling. 'What's going on here?' he asked.

'Don't take any notice of him,' said one of the inmates.
'He thinks he's a light-bulb.'

'Well,' said the superintendent with a smile, 'I'll soon
take care of that. I'll just turn him off!'

He stepped over to the wall switch and one of the other
patients shouted, 'Hey, wait a minute! How do you expect
us to work in the dark?'

How many NUCLEAR POWER STATION PLANNERS does it
take to change a light-bulb?

*Ten. One to change the bulb and nine to work out how to
dispose of the old bulb for the next 20,000 years.*

How many HI-FI salesmen does it take to change a light-
bulb?

*One – 'But I'm afraid they don't make that model any more,
sir.'*

How many SHOP ASSISTANTS does it take to change a
light-bulb?

*One – but he'll only change it if you have the receipt for the old
one.*

How many IRISHMEN does it take to change a light-bulb?

Six. One to change the bulb and five to turn the ladder round and round.

How many NEW AGE TRAVELLERS does it take to change a light-bulb?

Only one – but first he has to steal a light-bulb.

How many HOSPITAL DOCTORS does it take to change a light-bulb?

Twenty. One to change the bulb and nineteen to complete the necessary paperwork.

A man was standing at the top of a very tall ladder, changing a light-bulb. Suddenly he slipped and crashed to the ground.

'Are you all right?' asked his wife anxiously. 'Did the fall hurt you?'

'No, it wasn't the fall that hurt me,' he replied. 'It was the abrupt stop. It was actually rather lucky that the ground broke my fall.'

How many CONSERVATIVE POLITICIANS does it take to change a light-bulb?

Only one – but the bulb must be manufactured by his own company, of which he is the (undisclosed) managing director.

How many SOFTWARE ENGINEERS does it take to change a light-bulb?

None. Changing a light-bulb is a hardware problem.

How many ROCK AND ROLL SOUND ENGINEERS does it take to change a light-bulb?

'Did you say something?'

How many HOLLYWOOD FILM STARS does it take to change a light-bulb?

Just one – but he only takes one step up the ladder, and then his stunt double takes over to complete the job.

How many IRISHMEN does it take to change a light-bulb?

Two. One to change the bulb and one to read out the instructions.

An Irishman was sent to change a light-bulb in an office lift. He saw a notice which read: THIS LIFT IS FOR SIX PERSONS ONLY. He waited an hour and a half for five other people to show up.

How many COUNCIL MAINTENANCE MEN does it take to change a light-bulb?

'Sorry, it can't be done. We just don't have the funds for non-essential work.'

How many CARLTON TELEVISION STAFF does it take to change a light-bulb?

Two. One to change the bulb and one to film the electrocution.
(RORY BREMNER)

How many MODERN ARTISTS does it take to change a light-bulb?

Two. One to change the bulb and one to sell the old one mounted on a gold-plated brick in a goldfish bowl to the Tate Gallery for £20,000, and entitled 'Is God Dead?'

How many SLOANE RANGERS does it take to change a light-bulb?

Two. One to mix the gin and tonic and one to phone Daddy.

How many CAR-DEALERS does it take to change a light-bulb?

Two. One to change the bulb and one to arrange a trade-in deal on the old one.

In the old days of the Soviet Union, a businessman visited Moscow on a trade mission. Having heard all about the KGB, and being of a suspicious nature, the first thing he did was to search his bedroom carefully to see if there were any hidden microphones or bugging devices. Directly under his bed he noticed some suspicious-looking wires, so he got out his nail scissors and cut through them. Next morning at breakfast, the waiter said, 'Did you hear about the very strange thing that happened last night, sir? The chandelier in the hall fell down!'

How many PSYCHIATRISTS does it take to change a light-bulb?

One – but the bulb must really want to change.

How many HOME OFFICE OFFICIALS does it take to change a light-bulb?

Four. One to change the bulb and three to instal the bugging equipment.

How many ENTHUSIASTS does it take to change a light-bulb?

'*It's changed!*'

How many TELEVISION ART DIRECTORS does it take to change a light-bulb?

'*Does it have to be a light-bulb? I think perhaps a chandelier would look better – or perhaps just a simple candle . . .*'

What would a Red Indian say if you asked him to change a light-bulb?
'How?'

How many STUNTMEN does it take to change a light-bulb?

Four. One to change the bulb and three to put the mattresses round the bottom of the ladder for when he falls off.

How many ROMAN CATHOLICS does it take to screw in a light-bulb?

Two. One to do the screwing and one to hear his confession.

How many JUNKIES does it take to change a light-bulb?

'Change the light-bulb? You mean it's, like, blown, and everything's, like, dark?'

How many INHABITANTS OF SARAJEVO does it take to change a light-bulb?

'What's a light-bulb?'

How many JAPANESE TOURISTS does it take to change a light-bulb?

Twenty. One to change the bulb and nineteen to take photographs of the event.

How many MAFIA HIT-MEN does it take to change a light-bulb?

They never do. They're afraid of injuring their trigger-fingers.

What's the difference between a light-bulb and a pregnant woman?
You can unscrew a light-bulb.

If there had been light-bulbs in Ancient Egypt, how many EGYPTIAN PHAROAHS would it have taken to change a light-bulb?

None. They'd have asked their Mummy to do it.

How many LAWYERS does it take to change a light-bulb?

How many can you afford?

How many GARAGE MECHANICS does it take to change a light-bulb?

'We'll have an estimate ready for you by the end of the month.'

How many COMPUTER PROGRAMMERS does it take to change a light-bulb?

At least two. One always changes jobs in the middle of the project.

Two taxi-drivers were changing a light-bulb in their hut at the cab rank. One of them handed up a 500-watt bulb to his mate, who said, 'Haven't you got anything smaller?'

How many SUMO WRESTLERS does it take to change a light-bulb?

You should never let a Sumo Wrestler change a light-bulb, he's far too big and clumsy. But then again, who's going to tell him?

How many CHAIN-SMOKERS does it take to change a light-bulb?

None. They've no need for light-bulbs – they're always lit up anyway.

How many FOOTBALLERS does it take to change a light-bulb?

Eleven. One to do the job and ten to throw their arms around him and give him a kiss.

How many ITALIANS does it take to change a light-bulb?

Three. One to hold the ladder, one to screw in the bulb and one to bribe the mayor for a permit.

How many POLISH BALLET GROUPS does it take to change a light-bulb?

None. They prefer Danzig in the dark.

How many STAR TREK CREW MEMBERS does it take to change a light-bulb?

Ten. When the light-bulb in the engine-room burns out, Scotty reports to Captain Kirk. Kirk checks and discovers that they have no spare light-bulbs. He stops in orbit at the next inhabited planet and beams down with Spock, Bones, Sulu and five crew members to borrow a bulb from the inhabitants. On landing, they are attacked and the five crew members are killed. Kirk and the others are captured. The inhabitants are stuck in a time-warp in the late twentieth century. Scotty reports that a Klingon warship is approaching the Enterprise on an attack course and he cannot take evasive action because without the light-bulb he can't see his instruments. The emperor of the planet is suffering from measles and Bones cures him. The grateful emperor gives Kirk a light-bulb and the party beams up to the Enterprise just in time to destroy the Klingon ship.

What did the police sergeant say when asked by his superior how the light-bulb over the reception desk at the station came to be smashed?

'Nothing to do with us, sir. It fell down the stairs all by itself.'

How many MARKET GARDENERS does it take to change a light-bulb?

Just one – but he always does it first thing in the morning because he likes to get his bulbs in early.

How many THIRD-WORLD CONSERVATIONISTS does it take to change a light-bulb?

They've got no time to change light-bulbs – they've got a whole planet to change.

How many CHINESE does it take to change a light-bulb?

One million – because, as Confucius say, 'Many hands make light work!'

How many GYNAECOLOGISTS does it take to change a light-bulb in the front hallway?

One – but he does it by putting both hands through the letter-box.

How does a Red Indian chief know that a light-bulb is faulty?
By the smoke signals it sends up.

How many DENTISTS does it take to change a light-bulb?

Two. One to extract the old bulb from its socket and one to administer the anaesthetic.

How many INHABITANTS OF CHERNOBYL does it take to change a light-bulb?

With inhabitants of Chernobyl around, who needs light-bulbs?

How many LOCAL COUNCILLORS does it take to change a light-bulb?

Thirty. Ten to set up a steering committee, ten to form a finance and audit committee, five to draft an official report and five to form a sub-committee to bypass the maintenance department and farm the work out to a private company.

How many FILM TECHNICIANS does it take to change a light-bulb?

'Nineteen.'
  'Nineteen?'
  'It's in the contract. Do you have a problem with that?'

How many SOCIOLOGISTS does it take to change a light-bulb?

'There are three current theories on this . . .'

How many ACTORS does it take to change a light-bulb?

Four. One to actually do it and three to stand around saying, 'Larry would have done it better.'

What's Harry Secombe's favourite light-bulb?
A sixty-watt-watt-watt-watt-watt-watt-watt!

How many ULTRA-CONSERVATIVE POLITICIANS does it take to change a light-bulb?

Just one – if you can explain to him why it needs changing in the first place.

How many US MARINES does it take to change a light-bulb?

Fifty. One to change the bulb and forty-nine to guard him and accidentally shoot several of the bystanders.

How many TRANSCENDENTAL MEDITATIONISTS does it take to change a light-bulb?

They never do. They just sit around in a circle, chanting their mantras, and the bulb changes itself.

How many ESTATE AGENTS does it take to change a light-bulb?

They don't. They draft an advertisement saying: 'Delightful, well-situated, luxury, period light-bulb in ground floor flat, in Adam-style lounge; suitable for reconversion into individually designed neo-Georgian light-bulb.'

Prime Minister John Major claims that there is light at the end of the tunnel. Do you ever get the feeling that it's just an oncoming train?

How many CONJURORS does it take to change a light-bulb?

One. Plus one gorgeous, scantily clad female assistant to divert attention so no one can see how he does it.

How many PERFORMANCE ARTISTS does it take to change a light-bulb?

Four. One to change the bulb, one to juggle the eggs, one to peddle the unicycle and one to time the whole procedure with a fish and a vacuum-cleaner.

How many COMPUTER DATA-BASE ANALYSTS does it take to change a light-bulb?

Three. One to write the light-bulb removal programme, one to write the light-bulb insertion programme and one to make sure that no one else tries to change the light-bulb in the meantime.

How many BANKERS does it take to change a light-bulb?

Six. One to hold the bulb and five to try to remember the combination.

How many LIBERALS does it take to change a light-bulb?

One. But only after consultation with thirty delegates representing ethnic minorities, women, gays, lesbians, battered wives, environmentalists . . .

How many THATCHERITES does it take to change a light-bulb?

They don't bother. They just leave it to market forces.

The Federation of British Industry recently decided to hold a 'Buy British' weekend to promote the British manufacturing industries. They arranged an outdoor gala banquet for the last evening, which was to be held in Hyde

Park. A vast marquee was erected and the surrounding area was decorated with thousands and thousands of coloured light-bulbs. The whole thing looked splendid, a glittering mass of twinkling lights. Only one thing spoiled the effect. A closer inspection of the light-bulbs revealed that each one was stamped MADE IN TAIWAN.

How many GRADUATE STUDENTS does it take to change a light-bulb?

One – and a professor to take the credit.

How many POETS does it take to change a light-bulb?

Three. One to curse the darkness one to light a candle and one to change the bulb.

How many MARXIST LENINISTS does it take to change a light-bulb?

None. The light-bulb contains the seeds of its own revolution.

How many IRANIANS does it take to change a light-bulb?

Twenty. One to change the bulb and nineteen to hold the house hostage.

It has been said that the legendary footballer Bobby Moore was so fast that when he retired for the night he could turn out the light and be back in bed before the room got dark.

How many MALE CHAUVINIST PIGS does it take to change a light-bulb?

None. 'Let the bitch cook in the dark!'

How many EFFICIENCY EXPERTS does it take to change a light-bulb?

None. Efficiency experts only replace dark bulbs.

How many GAG-WRITERS does it take to change a light-bulb?

Two. One to change the bulb and one to write twenty jokes beginning, 'There were these two Irishmen trying to change a light-bulb . . '

The holiday camp had a very strict rule. The staff were strictly forbidden to have visitors of the opposite sex in their chalets after ten o'clock at night. One evening, a lady Red Coat invited a male guest round to her chalet and, after a few drinks and a pleasant chat, she said, 'Well, it's almost ten o'clock – you'd better get going.'

'OK,' said the young man. 'Turn out the lights and we'll get started.'

How many SAS MEN does it take to change a light-bulb?

Twenty-five. One to change the bulb and twenty-four to repair the damage to the house.

How many MEMBERS OF GREEN PEACE does it take to change a light-bulb?

Six. One to change the bulb and five to write the environmental report.

How many FAMILY SOLICITORS does it take to screw in a light-bulb?

Family solicitors don't screw light-bulbs. They screw divorcees.

A policeman patrolling the streets of Dublin late one winter's night noticed a man on his hands and knees under a lamp-post. 'And what might you be up to?' he asked.

'Sure, I've dropped a ten-pound note, constable,' explained the man, 'and I'm trying to find it.'

'Are you sure you dropped it here?' asked the policeman.

'No – I dropped it somewhere in the next street,' said the man.

'Then what the devil are you looking in this street for?' said the policeman.

'Because the light's better here,' replied the Dubliner.

How many RUGBY PLAYERS AFTER WINNING A MATCH does it take to change a light-bulb?

Ten. One to change the bulb and nine to pull the ladder out from under him and smash the room with it.

How many PENTAGON HAWKS does it take to change a light-bulb?

One million and one. One to change the bulb and one million to try to rebuild civilization.

How many SOUTH AMERICAN PRESIDENTS does it take to change a light-bulb?

Nobody knows. South American presidents don't last as long as light-bulbs.

How many HASSIDIC JEWS does it take to change a light-bulb?

None. There will never be another light-bulb that burned as brightly as the first one.

The light-bulb over the desk of a big business executive was faulty and a maintenance man was sent to change it. The businessman became a little annoyed when the maintenance man clambered on to his desk in his filthy boots.

'Would you like a newspaper to stand on?' he asked.

'No, it's OK,' said the electrician. 'I can reach it from here.'

How many SHOP ASSISTANTS does it take to change a light-bulb?

'I'm on my lunch-break – ask the girl over there.'

How many EVOLUTIONISTS does it take to change a light-bulb?

Only one – but it takes him thirty million years.

How many SPANIARDS does it take to change a light-bulb?

Juan.

Can Bobby Fischer, CHESS GRAND MASTER, change a light-bulb?

Yes, he can – but it sometimes takes him an hour to make the first move.

How many CHINESE WORKERS does it take to change a light-bulb?

One. But a thousand troops are also needed in case he tries to go on strike.

The man was bleeding profusely from one ear when he came into the emergency room at the hospital. 'I bit myself,' he said to the nurse. 'I was changing a light-bulb and I bit myself!'

'Impossible!' said the nurse. 'How could you bite yourself on the ear?'

To which the man replied, 'I was standing on a chair.'

Conversations on the subject of light-bulb changing with famous personalities, past and present

ROGET, COMPILER OF THE FAMOUS 'THESAURUS'

'Mr Roget, how many workmen would it take to change a light-bulb?'
Normally, usually, as a rule, in most cases, it would take only one workman, artisan, artificer, technician, craftsman, menial, servant, operative or factotum to change, alter, replace, re-affix, renew, transform, regenerate or metamorphose one light-bulb or . . . er . . . I'm sorry, I can't think of another word for "light-bulb".'

NAPOLEON

'What would you say if Josephine asked you to change a light-bulb?'
'Not tonight, Josephine.'

MAE WEST

'Miss West, why did you replace all your forty-watt bulbs with hundred-watt ones?'
'So you could come up and see me some time, honey!'

CILLA BLACK

'Miss Black, do you enjoy changing light-bulbs?'
'Yes, *chuck – it's a lorra lorra laughs!*'

JOANNA LUMLEY

'Miss Lumley, how did your bedroom look after you had changed all the light-bulbs?'
'*Absolutely fabulous!*'

SHERLOCK HOLMES

'Mr Holmes, do you employ any special techniques when changing a light-bulb?'
'*No, it's elementary, my dear fellow.*'

WINSTON CHURCHILL

'Mr Churchill, in an emergency, could you and members of your War Cabinet change a light-bulb?'
'*Give us the tools and we will finish the job!*'

ALBERT EINSTEIN

'Mr Einstein, how would you change a light-bulb?'
'*Well, the whole question is relative, isn't it?*'

HER MAJESTY THE QUEEN

'Your Majesty, how many workmen would it take to change a light-bulb?'
'One, one would imagine, wouldn't one?'

JOHN MAJOR

'Prime Minister, how many workmen does it take to change a light-bulb?'
'In the short term, the fact of the matter is that, at the end of the day, the Government can't afford to rush into this sort of activity without due consultation with all parties concerned. Manning levels in unskilled trades must be cost-effective, especially in labour-intensive industries, but the government has invested over two billion pounds in . . .'
'Mr Major, will you please answer the question!'
'One.'

TERRY WAITE

'Mr Waite, how many Lebanese does it take to change a light-bulb?'
'I've no idea. They always blindfolded me before changing a light-bulb.'

SAMUEL GOLDWYN (FILM PRODUCER)

'Mr Goldwyn, how would you describe the operation of changing a light-bulb?'
'In two words – im-possible!'

MADONNA

'Do you need any help in screwing in a new light-bulb?'
'Where screwing is concerned, honey, I don't need no help from nobody!'

JOHN McENROE

'Mr McEnroe, have you ever changed a light-bulb?'
'You cannot be serious!!'

RHETT BUTLER (*Gone with the Wind*)

'Mr Butler, who changes the light-bulbs in your house?'
'Frankly, my dear, I don't give a damn!'

GILLIAN SHEPHARD *(Education Secretary)*

'Could you tell me how many workmen it takes to change a light-bulb?'
'Well, let's look at it this way. If it takes six men forty-seven minutes to change eighteen light-bulbs, how many men would it take to change one light-bulb in three minutes? Of course, under the proposed changes to the National Curriculum, such questions are no longer asked. Archaic knowledge of this kind can be of no possible use to the modern child.'

SAMUEL PEPYS

'Mr Pepys, I understand that when you tried to change a light-bulb, there was a slight accident?'
'Slight? Have you ever heard of the Great Fire of London. . . ?'

WINSTON CHURCHCHILL (AGAIN)

'Mr Churchill, what happened when you attempted to change a light-bulb in the War Room?'
'Blood, sweat, toil and tears!'

FRANCIS DRAKE

'Sir Francis, what did you say when your wife asked you when you were going to change the light-bulb?'
'Right after I've finished just one more game of bowls, my dear . . .'

PAUL DANIELS

'Mr Daniels, do you enjoy changing light-bulbs?'
'*Not a lot!*'

WILL THE LAST PERSON TO READ

THIS BOOK

PLEASE TURN OUT THE LIGHTS.